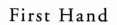

First Hand

ALSO BY LINDA BIERDS

The Seconds (2001)

The Profile Makers (1997)

The Ghost Trio (1994)

Heart and Perimeter (1991)

The Stillness, the Dancing (1988)

Flights of the Harvest-Mare (1985)

First Hand

poems

. . .

Linda Bierds

A MARIAN WOOD BOOK
Published by G. P. Putnam's Sons
a member of Penguin Group (USA) Inc.
New York

A MARIAN WOOD BOOK
Published by G. P. Putnam's Sons
Publishers Since 1838
a member of the Penguin Group
Penguin Group (USA) Inc., 375 Hudson Street, New York, New York 10014, USA •
Penguin Group (Canada), 10 Alcorn Avenue, Toronto, Ontario M4V 3B2, Canada
(a division of Pearson Penguin Canada Inc.) • Penguin Books Ltd, 80 Strand, London
WC2R 0RL, England • Penguin Ireland, 25 St Stephen's Green, Dublin 2, Ireland (a division
of Penguin Books Ltd) • Penguin Group (Australia), 250 Camberwell Road, Camberwell,
Victoria 3124, Australia (a division of Pearson Australia Group Pty Ltd) • Penguin Books
India Pvt Ltd, 11 Community Centre, Panchsheel Park, New Delhi–110 017, India •
Penguin Group (NZ), Cnr Airborne and Rosedale Roads, Albany, Auckland 1310, New
Zealand (a division of Pearson New Zealand Ltd) • Penguin Books (South Africa) (Pty) Ltd,
24 Sturdee Avenue, Rosebank, Johannesburg 2196, South Africa
Penguin Books Ltd, Registered Offices:
80 Strand, London WC2R 0RL, England

Library of Congress Cataloging-in-Publication Data

Bierds, Linda.
First hand : poems / Linda Bierds.
p. cm.
"A Marian Wood book."
ISBN 0-399-15261-X
1. Science—Poetry.   2. Scientists—Poetry.   I. Title.
PS3552.I357F47   2004   2004055298
811'.54—dc22

Printed in the United States of America
3   5   7   9   10   8   6   4   2

This book is printed on acid-free paper. ∞

For my brother

Grateful acknowledgment is made to the following magazines, where these poems first appeared, some in slightly different form: *The Atlantic Monthly*: "Questions of Replication: The Brittle-Star"; *Field*: "The Monarchs," "Time and Space"; *Gulf Coast*: "Prodigy," "Sans Merci"; *The Journal*: "Ecstasy," "On Color Vision Through a Prism," "Tulips, Some Said"; *The Kenyon Review*: "Gregor Mendel and the Calico Caps," "Gregor Mendel in the Garden," "Sext: Gregor Mendel and the Bells," "Terce: Gregor Mendel and Script"; *New England Review*: "Elegance," "Percussion," "Spillikins: Gregor Mendel at the Table"; *The New Yorker*: "Nineteen Thirty-four"; *TriQuarterly*: "Matins: Gregor Mendel and the Bees," "Stroke," "Thinking of Red"; *The Virginia Quarterly*

Review: "DNA," "Gregor Mendel and the Cats," "Vespers: Gregor Mendel and Steam."

I am grateful as well to the John D. and Catherine T. MacArthur Foundation, for its generous support. And, as always, to Marian Wood.

Author's Note and Acknowledgments

As they trundle through the centuries, swaying this way and that, from wonder to foreboding, the poems in this book rest most frequently at the inscape of science. It is there, in that innermost space lit by the nature of human achievement, that their interest and questions lie, their praise and disquietude.

An inquiry such as this, which moves from third-century-B.C. theories of buoyancy to twenty-first-century biochemistry, must acknowledge what are for many the global and spiritual implications of a science increasingly adept at creating, extending, and annihilating life. To help me with that task, I've turned to the character of Gregor Mendel, whose work on the hybridization of peas foreshadowed genetic cloning. Mendel, for years carefully capping in calico his newly impregnated pea blossoms, labored at

Saint Thomas Monastery, in Moravia, where he lived as a monk from 1843 until his death in 1884. Augustinian in its habits, the monastery encouraged research, which often included the cross-breeding of plants and animals. This activity, advancing for the monks an understanding of the complexities of Creation, was seen by the monastery to be completely compatible with worship. Others disagreed.

My familiarity with Mendel's life, the texture and conflicts of his times, was greatly increased by Robin Marantz Henig's immensely engaging *The Monk in the Garden* (Houghton Mifflin, 2001). Without its comprehensive history and love of detail, the Mendel of these poems—a projection, finally, of my imagination—could not have begun to exist.

Gratitude and acknowledgment are due as well to Steven Reynolds, the inspiration for my gloved guide in this book's penultimate poem, and to the Department of Biochemistry at the University of Washington in Seattle. There, on a winter morning in 2004, with the help of poet and biology student Jessica Johnson, I observed, deep within a living cell, the spindle-shaped figure along which chromosomes crawl during mitosis. Later that morning we went deeper, into the region at the figure's tip, a seemingly magnetic pole where the spindle's thin, longitudinal fibers met. To study that microcosmic world, to map its geography, Reynolds had infused the pole with green fluorescent protein—a green cloned from the body of a jellyfish—and I watched, at 1,200 times its size, the glow of its cartographic life.

Our instrument for magnification that morning cast its light upward to meet my downward gaze. Unlike the downcast light from my childhood microscope—flawed and companionable a few inches from my chin, its dusty path parallel to my own and the filament of its source chunky as Edison's oakum—the light from this scope seemed sourceless, unbidden, flawless, and infinitely precise, as indestructible in its journey as I was not. It seemed the future's harbinger as our gazes met and we held, in the fleeting grip of that meeting, the matter that lay between us.

—*LB, May 2004*

Contents

· · · *This symbol is used to indicate a space between stanzas
whenever such space is lost in pagination.*

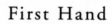

First Hand

Prologue

They darken. In the sky over Florence,
the oblong clouds swell and darken.
And hailstones lift back through the updrafts,
thickening, darkening, until, swollen as bird eggs,
they drop to the cobbled streets.

Horses! the child Galileo thinks, then
peeks through the doorway
to the shock of ten thousand icy hooves.
At his back, his father is tuning violins,
and because there is nothing sharper at hand

Galileo saws through a captured hailstone
with a length of E-string,
the white globe opening slowly, and the pattern inside
already bleeding its frail borders.
Layers and layers of ice—

Like what? Onion pulp? Cypress rings?
If only the room were colder, and the eye
finer. If only the hand were faster,
and the blade sharper, and firmer,
and without a hint of song . . .

PART ONE

· · ·

Time and Space

Deep space. The oblong, twinkle-less stars
matte as wax pears. And the astronauts are losing heart,
the heady lisp of auricle and ventricle
fading to a whisper, as muscles shrink to infants' hearts,
or the plum-shaped nubs of swans.
Atrophy, from time in space, even as the space in time
contracts. And how much safer it was—
ascension—at some earlier contraction, each flyer intact,

cupped by a room-size celestial globe
staked to a palace lawn. How much easier, to duck
with the doublets and powdered wigs
through the flap of a trapdoor and watch on a soot-stained
copper sky the painted constellations, or,
dead-center, a fist of shadowed earth dangling from a ribbon.

All systems go, of course: each moist,
diminishing heart, just sufficient at its terminus to fuel
the arm, the opening hand, to coax
to the lips a fig or pleated straw. Still, how much easier
to drift in a hollow globe, its perpetual,
tallow-lit night, while outside with the mazes and spaniels
. . .

the day, like an onion, arced up in layers
to the dark heavens. How much safer to enter a time, a space,
when a swan might lift from a palace pond
to cross for an instant—above, below—its outstretched
Cygnus shape, just a membrane
and membrane away. A space in time when such accident
was prophecy, and such singular alignment—
carbon, shadow, membrane, flight—sufficient for the moment.

Counting:
Gregor Mendel in the Prelacy

My companions since childhood, these numbers.
My constant counterparts, as lime kilns
steamed on our green hills

and my father grafted to russet knuckles
a golden apple's fingerlings. (That first stalk
six posts from the gate, and the gate
twelve strides from the pond.)

Each winter, I loved the ermine's harmony,
how it stitched over fresh drifts
the parallel pricks of its tracks. And the pale,

symmetrical petals of snow, how they covered
our seventy houses, our eight hundred
yoke of good arable, good meadowland,
our four hundred ninety souls.

Holy Father, do not think that I think of you less
when I think of you mathematically.
. . .

Tomorrow, November closes—
and, polished by frost, the church bells
respond with a clarity. Already,

one-fourth of the compost
is eaten by lime, one-third of the belfry
by shadow. How the second hand ticks!
Stay with me, now, as I wind through my first life. . . .

Elegance

Not Archimedes, naked and tufted, still wet from his bath,
screaming "Eureka" through the streets of Syracuse,
but the insight that propelled him, that sudden proof,
that buoyant, blushed epiphany. *Elegance*
they call it, the long-boned mathematicians,

when facts align like alloys on a balance scale.

For the slender Archimedes, the scale tipped
eleven stones. Yet once within the tub's cool grip
several stones departed, skipped suddenly away,
soundlessly, invisibly, as the soul's clear micro-ounce

is said to skip across death's placid water.

Then, as he sank, the weight he seemed to lose emerged:
The bathtub's water overflowed in perfect shares of
Archimedes. And so, from principles of buoyancy:

Elegance. And a running man.

Someone draped him in a linen sheet,
then watched him disappear

. . .

within a stone, linen-tinted passageway—a melded shape

across the stairs, the rubbled walls, where lantern smoke
cast its rubbled soot. Twenty centuries would pass

before a taper maker, weighted

with years of weightless ash, would blend
the sootless, smokeless candle, and cleanse the walls
where Archimedes walked. His secret

lay with feasting—a feed for bees

so balanced in its elements of sharp and sweet,
of oil and air, that the buoyant, tufted bodies
churned out from their chambered furnaces a kind
of waxy catalyst—a flawless stitch from mass to light.

Honey. Lentils. Two yellow wines. Two mackerel skins.
. . .

Elegant, that formula, that sudden click of harmony
when facts aligned, and matter, from the bee or from
the bath, lost not itself but simply its perimeter.
Elegant, that sudden shift beyond the eye, that soundless
click: clear stone across some greater clarity.

Matins:
Gregor Mendel and the Bees

Slowed by smoke, they slump
from the hive,
benign from the hive they slump,
Father of thorax and wing,
Father of light, they light
on my arm, make light
of my arm, tapering, golden,
Father of darkness receding,
they make from my arm
a candle, a flame, they candle
my arm with backcast
light, affixing the self
to the shell.

The Trinity Years

Sharp-eyed, slim-toed, a hawk through the woodwork
of Trinity College, the young Isaac Newton
entered in shorthand a list of his sins, each crimped cipher
gracefully sloped—*n* for *not*, *bef* for *belief*, as in

   Not living according to my belief

Then in longhand's boxy script—a nod
toward expansion perhaps—he penned with flourish
Certain Philosophical Questions:

   WHITHER FIRST MATTER BY MATHEMATICAL POINTS
   OR MATHEMATICAL POINTS AND PARTS

The list of his sins stitched the past—

   Peevishness with my mother

—to the present—

   Using Wilford's towel to spare my own

. . .

—while his questions stepped off toward timelessness:

WHY WATER IS CLEARER THAN VAPORS
WHY OBJECTS APPEAR TO BE OUTSIDE OUR BODIES

Slowly, the Heavens shifted. Rain. A brief snow.
Ale mugs swelled with an amber foam; teacups clicked down
on their saucers. He walked in his dark robes,
kicking a stone, tracking the stars. . . .

> *Glutony*
> *Striving to cheate with a brass half crowne*
> WHY REFRACTION IS LESS IN HOT WATER THAN COLD
> WHITHER MAGNETIC RAYS WILL BLOW A CANDLE
> WHITHER ACUTE OR GRAVE SOUNDS ARE THE SWIFTER
> *Lying about a louse*

And what of the sea? The air? The soil? What of fire,
fantasy, sapors, sleep? Yes, what of sleep, with the day
too short in its hours, the week too short in its days?
What of wonder? Piety? The clash of desire and reverence?

> *Making a feather pen on Thy day.*
> *Making a mousetrap on Thy day.*
> *Twisting a cord, contriving the chimes, making a water watch—*
> *on Thy day.*

. . .

And how, despite the day, could the Heavens reject
those twisted cords and feather pens, those
ceaseless meditations, *heating the braine to distraction*?

How, in light of Creation's complexity, could devotion
stand free from inquiry, vast love from articulation?

His list stopped. At the hour hand's tapered gate
the Questions crowded like cattle. How rich
the world's meadow! And the rolling, seed-strung galaxy!
How persistent the lowing! (How less swift than the bray?)
Here was the Universe: ale mugs and beakers,
plum stones and orbs, the delicate, finite, human body,
its lips and heated braine, its fingertips, slipping a towel
from a wooden rack, its magnet-filled palms,
torquing light toward the coming world.

WILL REFLECTION . . . WILL REFLECTION
UNRIDDLE THE MYSTERY OF THE COMET'S BIRD?

Scholars say he meant "beard," that figurehead light
preceding a comet's nucleus. Still, he wrote "bird." Twice.
As if, through reflection, a form unfolded
its gangly wings, whirled and unfolded
its gangly wings—because something larger,
wild for islands in mystery's flood,
cupped its dormant shape, then sent it flying.

Prodigy

Lovely, he thinks, stepping off from the shoreline,
how the pond erases his shadow
in equal proportion
to the body its water accepts. Until, as shadow,
he is nothing, just head and an upraised arm—
while, pale in the pond, he is Benjamin Franklin,
a child with a kite on a string.

And now he is cargo, drawn by the wind,
as pond water slaps
and the kite's red gills billow. Such pleasure,
shoulders to toes, all
down the slim, cirrus shape of his body,
to be pulled by the wind, half fish, half bird,

while horse carts clack down the Boston streets, deep
in their own progress, and shadows
slip westward, and the long fingers of tallow,
pale in his father's shop, dip and thicken and dip.

Blue day. On the salt marsh hills, other boys play out
their landlocked strings, crisscrossing
the grasses, heavy as pendulums. Only one,
young Franklin, floats with his kite,

. . .

weightless and tethered in equal proportion.
White-knuckled, good-natured, he would wave
if he could. But he is a staple
binding the elements. White knot
at the end of a stitch. And lovely, he thinks, to be
both the knot and the stitch. That
is the secret, isn't it? To be, at once,
all body, all soul. That is the key.

Thinking of Red

—Marie Curie, 1934

Back from the workbench and lamp, the tilt
of the microscope's mantis head, back from the droplet
of sea, salted by powdered radium,
and the lift and swirl of its atoms—the buffed,
invisible globes of its atoms—she sat
with her apple and knife, confined to her wide bed.

I am thinking of red, she said. And those
primary years, gathered like cardinals.
Although there were no cardinals, of course.
But gooseberries. And roe, there was roe
so gold it was red. All the fruit trees were padded
with cabbage leaves, and she climbed, red in her pinafore,

through their crackling branches. Now and then,
from the movements of children above her,
dry cabbage leaves rained a brittle parchment.
And then, just silence, as they sat with their meals
of bread and gooseberries—like mythic birds
in their bright aprons—while the Polish sun,

. . .

for miles to the west, cast to their pale,
partitioned land the fractured shadows of fruit trees.
Thinking of red . . . corpuscles, their freight of typhus,
their glowing freight of radium. But—no—today
just the red of those childhood years. Roe.
And apples, how the ships slipped down from Kasmierz,

laden with apples. Thin ships, so weighted they seemed
just prow, great horses legging the yellow river.
On deck, she would watch the straw raked back,
as the scent of a thousand russet apples—
nested like cardinals—rose in the winter air.
She could toss to the river the blemished ones—

the captain gave permission—then cover her basket
with perfect others, the red, chilled, perfect
globes, so cold they would fill the season.
But even the blemished lingered awhile,
lifted and dove through the clear air, and sent
to the prows and empty docks, to the winter rafts
. . .

and long horizon, their sets of concentric rings.
Before they sank through the closing water,
they lifted and turned as . . . atoms must. Or better,
cardinals. Although there were no cardinals,
of course, just flight and its watery echo, red
over red, over red, as far as the eye could see.

Gregor Mendel in the Garden

Black-robed on the green hillside,
he seems less shape than space—Abbot Napp—
a gap in a flock of April lambs.
Then wind opens his wide sleeves and the flock
scatters—his little ones, his progeny, bred, crossbred.

In this first morning light, I am turning
the garden, kneeling and rising, my apron flapping
its own dark wing. Such a daybreak of drops
and ascensions!—winter on the pebble, sunlight
on the nape, and the black soil swallowing

my pea seeds, like beads through a crow's gullet.
With grace and patience, the Abbot
would cancel in his scattered lambs
the parasites, the strucks and toxin shards
that yearly fell them. But life's eluded him

and so he breeds for beauty: a triple crimp in wool,
a certain glint in lanolin. And the spiral horn—
that curling cornucopia—corrugated, green-cast,
shaped, he says, by repetition's needs.
(*Not unlike your pea pods, Gregor.*)

. . .

Beautiful, he tells me, those circling, dusty pleats.
And if only he could breed there some brief
continuation. Another swirl, he says, another turn
on matter's slender axis. Another rise—*Gregor*—
another dip. Before the ripping tip.

Percussion

To tell the child, Gianlorenzo Bernini, why the purslane
bloomed so mysteriously, someone first had to tell
of the burning—how the heretic slumped

like a staked vine, while into the flames
a woman kept tossing softened figs, their hiss
and waxy collapse drawing the eye away and away.

And how, at the fire's rim, three boys rocked back
in their black saddles, each face stretched
to a hybrid mask: triumph and a caustic grief.

Then they lashed their horses through the Roman streets
and over a pale hill, their pathless, erratic paths
cracking the earth and dormant seeds. . . . And so,

from percussion, Bernini learned, three rivulets
of flowers bloomed, each yellow trail
jagged as the flight of a running boy.

Already, at ten, he had carved from marble
an infant and faun, his own percussion
bringing to stillness their shared movements. But there
. . .

on the hillside, tapping brought forth the opposite:
from the static seed a yellow trail, fluid
in the arid wind. Were there others, then—closed seeds—

near the lakes, the umbrella pines?
In how many ways might shape take shape?
He knew that sunset could stretch into ponds

the long shadows of oxen, or that swans and archers
could swell from the scattered stars.
He knew that fire had, for a moment,

unfolded the waxy fig, and the soul
of the heretic—Bruno—who believed the earth
was a simple star in a fabric

of infinite stars. Already, at ten,
he knew those shapes, those transformations.
But where were the other dormancies, tight

in the soil's vast rim? And what forces could possibly
open them, when the world he had witnessed
blossomed only from light?

PART TWO

. . .

Spillikins:
Gregor Mendel at the Table

On the table, a nest of fretted sticks:
trefoil, knife blade, horse head, bell,
snake on a staff, bird on a branch,
miter, bucket-yoke, fork.
And at my elbow, black tea,
the mahogany sheen of contentment.

All afternoon, to train the hand,
I lifted the snake from the branch,
the yoke from the horse,
the bird from the yoke,
each carved bone such weighted weightlessness.
And then, through the window, it came—

for a moment, through the window—
that silence so still it is holy. That stillness
when the world's swirl suddenly stops
and everything—wind and whinny and cough—
is gripped by respite's harmony.
Then the grip loosened
. . .

and all down the hillsides the church bells spilled.
And under the bells, the birds,
and under the birds, the metallic chitter
of knife blades, forks,
and I rose
for the body's sustenance.

Stroke

To stroke from stone the hovering bee—
to release from marble its white thorax—the hand
must turn back on itself, palm up, fingers curved,
with the gesture of skipping stones over water.
And to sculpt the wings, the hand must arc downward,
fingers stiff, with the gesture of rubbing grief
from the brow. And so, Gianlorenzo Bernini learned,
carving bees for the Pope's family shield, for the churches
and Roman fountains: palm up
in the workshop, palm up in the world; fingers stiff
on the chisel and brow; hand curved to the hammer,
hand curved to the wineglass; palms pressed
for the wafer, palm up for the thorax, the coin,
for the quick rains that washed from his skin
the decades of white dust.

To free Saint Teresa to her ecstasy, or Daphne
to her leafed future, the hand must know first
the promise of wax. Or graphite. Or the tepid flesh
of clay. The hand must know first
the model. These are the angles, Bernini said,
for the animate, human form: acute, obtuse,
salient, re-entering. Hour by passing hour,
his room filled with stone chips and ciphers,

the metallic scent of mathematics. Now and then,
a brief snow tempered his marble horses.
Now and then, migraine headaches made lace
of his world. These are the compasses, slipped
from their soft pouches. And these, the reflex angles
of their pivoting leg, when the hand, circling,
turns back on itself.

To curry from stone the texture of silk, or feathers,
or the fluid parchment of bee wings, the hand
must pursue the source, must open to fullness
the brief wing, or the downward slope
of the lover's robe, so that stone might turn back
on itself, might climb through the strata of bedrock
and centuries to echo the living—just as the living
climb down into stone. These are the hand strokes,
Bernini said: frontal, alee, emergent, re-entering.
For the climbing, shapes to their shaped reversals—
as, two days from his death, shapes would climb
through his right arm, through the long wick of his nerves:
little sparks, little Janus flames, lighting their own
departure. Then a thrum, he said. All through the flesh
that thrum. Bees. White bees.

Terce:
Gregor Mendel and Script

Quiet hour, the lamb in the field
and now on the page.
And the page itself the lamb,
fleshside and peltside.
Quiet hour, and now on the page
the lamb, and now of *the page*
the burnished lamb.
Sunlight. Day. The vessels
at one with their cargoes.
And I, Holy Father, pale shape
in this whitening hour?
Receive me as soapstone on glass,
released by breath: Gregor.

Sans Merci

Away, the maid called in her small voice,
and Severn pulled the tray away, up
on its polished ropes, up
from Rome's rain-washed Spanish Steps:
rabbit flanks on a pewter plate,
a linen napkin's cool meringue, all climbing
the inn's exterior wall, then pulled
through a window where Keats lay dying.
And down again, the residue—
bone shards and cloth, dappled by grease
and arterial blood. Up came the brisket
and boiled trout,
                    although, at last,
Keats favored the gleam that enclosed them,
the silver cloches and water flask,
the glint of the rope-cupped silver tray—
bright, steadfast star—eclipsing
the window's aperture. Away, he said,
then down by its ropes the untouched,
soft-fleshed shape swayed, ration

and glint, back toward the small-voiced maid—
beautiful, surely, in her dark cloak,
her hunger sharp but her step
light, as she turned past the inn's chilled wall
to ferret it all away.

Gregor Mendel
and the Calico Caps

With tweezers light as a pigeon's beak,
I have clipped from each stamen a pollen-filled anther:
hour by hour, three hundred tiny beads, dropped
in my robe's deep pocket, their yellow snuff
sealing the seam lines. And thus,

I emasculate peas that would sire themselves.

Heresy, some say,
to peel back the petal, sever the anther, stroke
to the open blossom—with the sweep of a pollen-tipped
paintbrush—another blossom's heritage.
Heresy, to mingle seed

fixed in the swirl of the world's first week.

Rest, now.
The bird-beak tweezers mute on my lap.
In France, where orchards yield to upswept Alps,
they have tied to the legs of pigeons
parchment memoranda—silk threads

encircling the flaccid skin, and a burl of words

. . .

that lifts between neighboring rooftops.
Twofold, I believe,
the gift of those gliding wings:
for the mind, script,
for the soul, the sluiced shape of the thermals,

at last made visible to the upturned eye . . .

My fingers are weary. Snuff in the seam lines.
To ward off the breeze and the bee,
I have tied to each blossom a calico cap. Three hundred
calico caps. From afar in this late-day light,
they nod like parishioners in an open field,

murmuring, stumbling slightly through the green expanse,

as I, in my labors, am stumbling. And all of them
spaced, it appears, on the widening arc
of some grand design. Blossom and cap in some
grand design. Vessel and motion and the tinted threads.
Heresy? Have I not been placed on that widening path?

Am I not, in my calling, among them?

DNA

At hand: the rounded shapes, cloud white, the scissors, sharp,
two dozen toothpick pegs, a vial of amber glue.
It's February, Cambridge, 1953,
and he's at play, James Watson: the cardboard shapes,

two dozen toothpick pegs, a vial of amber glue.
White hexagons, pentagons, peg-pierced at the corners—
he's at play, James Watson, turning cardboard shapes
this way, that. And where is the star-shot elegance

when hexagons, pentagons, peg-pierced at the corners,
slip into their pliant, spiral-flung alignments?
Where is that star-shot elegance? This way? That?
He slips together lines of slender pegs that quickly

split in two. (Pliant, spiral-flung, one line meant
solitude. But one to one? Pristine redundancy.)
He slips. Together, lines of slender pegs quickly
conjugate. White hexagons, white pentagons:

not solitude but—one, two, one—pristine redundancy.
So close the spiral shape, now. Salt and sugar atoms
congregate: white hexagons, white pentagons.
So close the bud, the egg, the laboratory lamb,

. . .

the salt and sugar atoms' spiral shape. So close—
it's February, Cambridge, 1953—
the blossom, egg, the salutary lamb. So close
at hand, the rounded shapes—cloud white—the scissors—sharp.

Questions of Replication:
The Brittle-Star

Why now, under seven fathoms of sea,
with sunlight just a sheen on its carapace
and someone's dark paddle stroking above?
Why, at this moment, does it lift from the reef
its serrated jaws, its four, undulant,
tendril arms—the fifth atomized
by a predator's nudge—to begin
the body's slow unbuckling? Near the reef,
a kick-dust of plankton hovers. And eelgrass.
And far down the sea floor, the true starfish
in their dank, illegible constellations.
What salt-rich analgesic allows
this self-division, as the disc parts
and tendril arms, each with a thousand
calcite eyes, sway into slender helixes?
Half disc and half disc. Limb pair; limb pair.
Two thousand eyes; two thousand crystal eyes—
that must notice now the emergent other,
aslant but familiar, slowly swimming away:
its butterflied, genetic list, its tendency
to luminescence. Limb over limb,
where is it headed? And when will its absence

echo, adrift in the sea's new weight?
Half shape; half shape—how far will it stroke
before loss, like daylight, lessens,
and the one that remains twines its optic arms
to look to the self for completion?

Ecstasy

It began, as it will, in privacy,
Hedy Lamarr, right hand on the ivory keys,
an octave below her, George Antheil, slim
on a leather bench. He was playing a riff.
She followed. Again, then again, impulse
and echo, call and response, and Look,
she whispered, we are talking in code,
our sweet locution seamless, unbreakable.

And just what the nation needed—they knew—
a secret-spun articulation, a ciphered
tête-à-tête. It was 1942,
radio signals simple and jammable.
Here was the answer: a ticking riff,
electric, magnetic, hopping the frequencies,
tapping its glossy fingertips
down a slumped torpedo's salty flank.

Out through the century its spectrum spread,
battlefield to microchip, a million million
cryptic trysts—while Lamarr with her patent,
her prize, met in darkness her flickering other.
Emulsion and light, she was less than a girl,
onion-skin thin on a waxy screen.

And desire's perfect complement:
weightless, ageless, a film on the upturned eye.

How innocent her image then, as out through
the century's cone-lit rooms, a nation sank
into velvet chairs. Then call and response,
synapse and blush, and Look, she whispered,
there is nothing between us—until nothing
stopped her airy touch, and nothing
stirred, and nothing cast its rhythmic clicks
high in the darkness above them.

Sunderance

Thin as swords, the five-foot corkscrew drills
gleamed on the fishermen's shoulders, eight hundred
    helixed blades, eight hundred fur-capped men
crossing the pack ice, three, four, five miles from shore,
    as the far spires of St. Petersburg
slipped under the earth's rim, and the shore fringe
    of birch slipped under, until only
ice and horizon remained. Just hue lines,
    sky and sea, white ice and a lesser ice,
pocked as citrus skin—an air-rich, smelt-rich slate
    where they set their drills, their lines, then crouched
into low chairs. And soon it began,
    someone said: a trembling, a low, locomotive
grumble. And they rose together, eight hundred thick
    in a futile flock, as the grumble played out
and their pocked slate cracked from pack ice

*

    to lumber seaward in the offshore wind.
All day, all night, helicopters dropped
    their wire hammocks, and no one was lost,
though the floe fractured, then fractured again,
    and the flock split, re-split, until only
a few remained, facedown on their single pallets.

Each clung to a penknife fixed in the ice—
Lest we slip from those chips, one said, those motes

*

afloat in God's compound eye. Except earth was not
the body of God—he knew that now—not earth
   or the chipped heavens, or the low, locomotive
amplitudes, crisscrossing the iced horizon—

*

and all that was mercy could be forged firsthand:
those double blades that thwacked all night above him

*

and the single one that wed him to the ice.

The Monarchs

The linen scales of the butterflies' wings
catch and absorb this February rain
exactly as starched napkins
might blot the drift of an evening's spilled port.
Or, better, ale, for these are monarch butterflies,
more ocher than red. Two hundred million, caught

by the sudden freeze that follows rain
in a Mexican forest of the twenty-first century.
Two hundred million
tablets of ocher ice, trembling a bit, then toppling

simultaneously, with the sound of a distant chandelier
rocked by a sudden wind. Beneath
its shifting, clicking tines, near that window
percussion opens, Bishop Berkeley leans back
from a table, blotting his ale with a linen napkin.
To be is to be perceived, he offers. And we are

secure in our being, perceived as we are
by God's mind. A mind, in fact—now rain
slants through the window—not unlike
this chandelier, vast, multifaceted,

. . .

each swaying tine of perception
ochered by candlelight, each swaying tine
a plane of reflection: our pipe smoke and rubicund faces,
the sideboard, courtyard, elm tree,
the ice just forming at the window ledge—
all held and beheld so steadfastly.

Sext:
Gregor Mendel and the Bells

Forbidden,
our two-stroke bells of mourning,
our cholera bells of mourning,
the toll of their tolling fearsome,
we are told, the toll of their tolling
despondency.
                    Holy Father, all day
sepals have slipped
to the glasshouse floor,
wing petals, keel petals, while in
through the orchard's Aeolian harp
your breath has offered
its consolation: not upstrokes,
not backstrokes—the bell's twinned rings—
but a thousand thousand
chime-shards, their singular
cacophony.
                    Hour by hour,
through the buffed Aeolian harp . . .
and forgive me, my God,
if I find in your influx
no patterning, as I find

in these downfalls no fixed design.
All day on the glasshouse floor:
anther, pollen, sepal, standard,
stigma, stigma, wing.

PART THREE

. . .

Redux

They darken. In the ponds and springs near Stuttgart,
the oblong newt eggs swell and darken, cells
and their daughters, afloat in a cytoplasmic bath,
splitting, re-splitting, until, swollen to fullness,
they stroke through the brimming world.

Milkweed, the scientist, Hans Spemann, thinks,
then peers through a microscope's steady beam
to a shoal of landlocked seeds.
At his back, his newborn stirs in a wicker pram.
And because there is nothing softer at hand

Spemann saws through a two-celled newt egg
with a length of the infant's hair,
the plump globe opening slowly, and the matter inside
already building its new borders.
Two, then. Two lives. And how many sires—

Hans Spemann thinks—and how many heirs?
If only the path were brighter, and the lens
finer. If only the hand were surer
and the blade sharper, and firmer,
and without the glint of time . . .

Errand

Old now, the nimble-thumbed technology
that brought her here, this common Dorset lamb,
relaxed in her shallow stall, buff-fleeced, wall-eyed,
her scissored, horizontal bite
idly working the grain. Past the gates
and sterile mangers, the bulbous heads of heat lamps
nodding like sunflowers in their spaced rows,
her mother—that is, her genetic double—
lolls at a water trough, dangling her face
near its glassy other.
                              Old now, reflection's lure:
to see beyond the self, the self.
Far down this compound's spackled halls,
a lab-coated worker peers over the rim
of a cell's smooth globe, then parts with a finger of light
its long, chromosomic grasses. Old now, reflection's
selfsame lure. And old, the century
that would have found him on his knees, parting
the earth for resemblances:
                              bloodroot and mandrake,
heartleaf, the liver-lobed hepatica—
each with its dusty errand: to close from death

the body it mirrored. Or there by the fence line,
through an outburst of blue, the lung-shaped leaves
of borage, to reopen the body to breath.

Gregor Mendel and the Cats

Up the monastery walls, the brewery's yeast-scent
huffles. And the dusty cat, stretched high
over warm stones, swings her blunt snout this way
and that, yeastward and monkward, from
release to salvation. In the bright sun
her irises, like shutters, close,
leaving just a strip of liquid glint, the pupil's
vertical box.

I am sleepless today, the cats of my childhood
mewling all night, their phantom shapes
alit on my ceiling. Cat backs, stretched, flexed,
cat tails in counterpoint. Such mystery,
to be of the body perpetually.

We are minds here. And hands. And a corporal longing
that finds release in . . . the kitchen's bounty:
braised cutlets, a rose-hip sauce balanced by vinegar!

Still trapped in promise, new pea vines are nothing
but binary leaves, dual lobes in a dark loam. . . .

Last winter, with a blue that wedded
oxblood and royalty,

we painted our bookcase backboards.
Great swaths of such vivid blue! Half sea, half ember,
behind the leather volumes.

Often, in dreams, I sit in our library's great expanse,
the abbot and brothers around me—
as they are in waking—
and the works of Aquinas, Kepler,
Linnaeus, Sophocles, open before us.
My dreams replace our bookcase backboards
with vivid glass, a haunted, oxblood blue, translucent
in that timelessness.
Through arched windows,

stained sunlight hovers,
and the parquet floor—as it does in waking—
gleams from the sweep of our woolen slippers.
But the light I am drawn to,
in dream after dream,
glows out from the bookcase shelves,
slender and patternless. A glass-cast, vertical,
feral blue, it shimmers from gaps
where the works of the mind are missing.

Desire

In autumn, 1879, on a day like today,
the physicist, Charles Vernon Boys,
touched to a spider's quiet web a silver tuning fork,
its long A swimming a warp line, up and up.
The hour's the same, the hemisphere,
and so the sunlight must have banked at this degree
across his buttoned sleeve, and the steady A
stroked a morning's molecules
much like these—although the note I hear
is organ-cast, cathedral-bound, and the sleeve
this sunlight banks across
drapes in tempera from a saint's clasped hands.

Godless in this god-filled room, I'm drawn less
to the saint's sacrificial fate than to the way
like instruments vibrate sympathetically,
or how this painter's ratio of bone to powdered umber
precisely captures a dove's blunt beak. I'm drawn
to his abidingness, the hands that slowly milked
egg white from its yolk, and ground the madder root,
and shaved the gold, and sealed it all
in a varnish skin (although the skin's a web now,
shot through with cracks).
. . .

Perhaps he whistled, low in his teeth,
a tuneless breath that dried the saint's wet eye to matte.
Perhaps he scraped the iris back, and built
the ground, and scraped again, to make the light
interior (then varnished it, to make the light eternal).
Propped on a garden bench, a C-fork buzzed, Boys said,
whenever the A was struck. And the spider whirled.
Then down a warp line, desire's leggy shadow
rushed—and rushed—scraping its beak
on the silver mass, silking the tines,
convinced until the last, Boys said,
all that hummed was food.

On Color Vision Through a Prism
—James Maxwell, 1871

Thus far you have witnessed, he said, white sunlight reveal

its banded rainbow. Let us try the effect, now, of mixing

two colors with a paintbrush of light. Then he twisted

a slitted filter and the spectrum vanished

from the white screen, blue stepping off,

violet, amber, until only red and green

remained. Great care must be taken, he said, to worry

the filter fastidiously, the slits slipping thusly, thusly,

until . . . yellow arises. Yellow. A hybrid sensation less

dark than its parts. Of course, wishing yellow, no painter

would marry his red to his green, but his is the world's

matter, and ours is a matter of mind (brilliant

with promise). Great care must be taken to worry the lens

judiciously, lest the spectrum reflect too completely

upon us, which, as you see, reveals a banded vacancy,

reveals, as you see, little hummocks of naught

absorbed by the backdrop before us.

Nineteen Thirty-four

Radiant, in the Paris sun, the clustered chairs
and canopies, the clustered leaves, one and one
and one—and down the boulevard, the circus tent
in a blowsy park, the Hospital, boulangeries,
the Institute where Curie turns, then takes
in her blackened, slender fingers a finger-shaped

tube of radiation. And the blue Atlantic, radiant,
the American shore, the gold-flecked palette
Paul Cadmus lifts. It is a midday and sundown
in March. He will paint on the flank of an acrobat
a gilded skin. She will stroke down the test tube
a ticking wand. There is sunlight on their sleeves,

as the equinox shifts and the pale-bricked house
of Physics throws open its smallest doors. Radiant,
the boulevards and shorelines, the peat fields, polders,
steeple tops, the Appalachians, Pyrenees,
the river-etched terraces of Warsaw.
And the circus tent with its acrobats, stern-faced

. . .

and gilded, circling the ring on their parallel horses.
Radiant, their sudden shape, like fission's sudden
pyramid: one on the shoulders of two, two
on the shoulders of four, four on the eight
pumping, glistening haunches, and the sixteen
polished hooves, mute in the swirling dust.

Vespers:
Gregor Mendel and Steam

Not plumes. Not plumes
from the teapot's throat.
But force, unseen, the space
between plume and throat—pure steam,
a cleft near the porcelain throat.
Nightfall on the teacup, the window,
the breaths of the winter ewes.
Nightfall. Nightfall. Dark breach
between breath and ewe.
And what force, what force, now,
will carry our dormant souls?
Not breath. Not cloud.
Not plume. Not plume. Not
shape—Holy Father—but gap.

Sonnet Crown for Two Voices

The glow, how can I express it? My god,
it lifts from protein flecks, up and across
this crafted lens. From flecks of nothingness,
enlarged twelve hundred times, its simple, cold
fluorescence lifts, green as early pea pods.
Like Mendel's progeny, it blinks across
the vines of probability, the sap-glossed
spindle threads. How Gregor would have swooned.

*

Again today, soft bandages entwine
my sodden legs: edema's finery.
I know, of course, Death draws his liquid kiss
along my soul, his tepid, sallow brine.
A monk, in love with nature's symmetry,
I complement that kiss. I rise to it.

I compliment the kiss. I'd rise to it
in time, my gloved guide says. These clumsy hands
could, in time, trace a cell's meridian
or dip into a nucleus a pipette's
tiny mouth. In time, I'd brush chromatic
residue throughout an egg cell's curved expanse—
but we're just setting slides today, kissing glass
to glass to glass, click by sterile click.

                              *

Symmetry. The ram's curled horn. The ermine's tracks.
The leaded windowpanes, mute now with snow.
The hourglass I turn, re-turn (the pressing
down, the rising up). Twin cones. Fused necks.
Its counterpart once toppled us, once blew
across my darkened room a single, flapping wing.

Across our darkened room, it flaps its single wing.
Magnified one hundred times, it skims the scope's
broad screen, dips between the waterweed. Protist,
he says. Not plant, not animal, its wing
a single cell, its cell a self, a kingdom
set apart, both intermediate and whole.
We turn away. Our task's to track the glow
again. A deeper world, fluorescent, green.

*

Midday, October, 1870.
Above, air currents from the west-northwest;
below, air currents from the south: a two-toned
cloud bank sparking. Then from the prelacy
I saw, through sudden hail, a helixed axis
glint. And then the two-coned mass: cyclone.

Out past a two-coned mass it glints, cyclone-
spun or flung by trembling chromatin
quaking through this microworld. Shifting spindles
make the cones; shifting slides—I fear—this windblown
scene. But what veers by, star-shaped, black? And thrown
by what? It's just a speck of retina,
of course. Light's one-celled ash. Vision's glinting
artifact, intermediate and whole.

*

One pressing down, one rising up. And one,
alone, black-robed in the prelacy, convinced
those counterwinds would cancel him, would catch
within their compound eye the black-robed mote
he would become. And still, the scientist
within me watched. I held the desk and watched.

The scientist within me watched the desk
withdraw, and then the scope's glass stage, and then
a pocked, nucleic wall, as down we spun,
the shapes that held the shapes all slipping back,
peripheral. And now, two dye-cast
spindle poles appear, magnetic discs that seem
to summon chromosomes, that seem to bend
the stuff of us: east-southeast, west-northwest.

*

Five seconds long. Its path three fathoms wide.
And through the glass it shot a chink that, until
then, had held the heavens back: an earthen span
of roof tile, flitting like a deadly bird.
Across my desk, it tapped its leaden trill.
Tick. Tick. Tick. Tick. Six inches from my hand.

Tick. Tick. Tick. Tick. Six inches from my hand,
the desk clock turns, but we're outside of time,
our movements inward, vertical, unaligned
with moving on. Within this polar land
a micro-Borealis glows, green-banded
through the protein globes. From jellyfish, my friend
has spliced genes for green fluorescence. They find
expression here, he says. As do we, firsthand.

*

Silence. Infernal symphony of bricks
and wind and breaking glass . . . quieted. At rest
against a wall, the flapping, asymmetric bird
was just a tile. And I, no longer parts—
heart or soul or watching eye—was just
a monk, released to love—again—the world.

A monk, released to love the world again—
how Mendel would have blossomed here. Reversed
astronomer, he'd chart these inmost
lights of us: sky-shapes expressed through scrims
of sea. And counting traits, he'd diagram
what shapes await us. As we do now—with dextrous
grace, my gloved friend boasts. (Although, in these frail years,
mere skill seems thin.) Not grace? he asks. Well, mercy, then.

*

Silence, then through the frost of shattered glass
an afterglow arose—or pressed—fully formed
but borderless. As I will be, the swirling world
subtracted from the I of me: wind, chalice,
heartbeat, hand . . . Weightless, measureless, but beautiful,
the glow. How can I express it, my God?

Epilogue:
Tulips, Some Said

When Abraham Ortelius fell in love with the world,
sometime in the autumn of 1560, and vowed to map
its grand expanse, its seas and serrated coastlines,
that the mind might hold, as it does an onion,
"the weighty, layered wholeness of it,"
a tulip was launched, from Constantinople's limpid port
toward the deep-water docks of Antwerp.
Still tucked in its fleshy bulb, it rode
with a dozen others, rising and falling
near the textile crates, as the ship slowly crossed
the southern sun, past Athens and Napoli, Elba, Marseille.
This is the world, Ortelius said, holding up to his friend,
Pieter Bruegel, a flattened, parchment, two-lobed heart.
And this, Bruegel answered, paint still damp
on his landscape of games, each with its broad-backed child.
It was an autumn of chatter and doubt, wonder
and grief and a quick indignation, sharp as linseed.
Slowly the ship tracked the Spanish coast, rising
and falling as the rains began, and the olives darkened,
and red-tunicked soldiers, increasing their numbers,
rode north toward Flanders. When the bulb
of a tulip is parted—its casing is also a tunic—
it reveals to the eye the whole of itself, all it will need,

like a zygote cell, to enter its own completion:
roots and pulp and, deep at the center,
leaves and a coil of bud.
That is the world, said Pieter. And that, said Abraham,
each beholding the other's expanse: on a single plane,
the oblong, passive hemispheres and, as if caught
by a closer eye, stocky, broad-backed, hive-strewn shapes,
alit in their grave felicity.
Mistaken for an onion, the bulb was roasted
near the Antwerp docks, then eaten with oil and vinegar.
Still new to the region, the others were buried in soil.
In Abraham's early folios, South America blooms
from its western shore, articulating a shape
that has yet to appear, while in Bruegel's dark painting,
a child on a hobbyhorse whips a flank of air.
Neither man lived to see, in 1650, at Nuremberg's
Peace Fair and Jamboree, fifteen hundred boys
on their wooden horses, fifteen hundred beribboned manes.
Watched from the highest balconies, they filled the square
like tulips, some said. Like soldiers, said others.
Although none could be seen completely. At last, all agreed,
they gave to the square a muted, ghostly atmosphere,
like the moods in medieval tapestries
that hold in quiet harmony violence and a trellised rose—

although the sun that day was bright, all agreed,
and the wind splendid and clear, as it carried
the taps of those wooden hooves, and lifted
the ribbons this way and that, this way and that,
until night, like the earth, covered them.